Wealth is for everyone

Also, by the author:

WHO TO MARRY: GOD'S DOSSIER ON YOUR MISSING PIECE

WHO AM I: RESOLVING THE IDENTITY CRISIS

WEALTH IS FOR EVERYONE

GOD'S WEALTH CREATION STRATEGIES

By

Jake Prince

With contributions from
Olubamike Fadipe

TABLE OF CONTENTS

PREFACE

This book is written to inspire all on the possibility of acquiring wealth. Its content explores the fine details of wealth creation by distilling and adapting strategies seen in life and nature.

It is not meant to replace mainstay materials which teach sound financial principles. Like caviar, it might not fill the tummy but it is a delight to taste!

Truly, wealth is for everyone.

FOREWORD

Jake and I have known each other for well over 20 years. His thoughts and actions through the years would qualify as intelligent. But there is one quality about him that makes him special, and this book portrays it so well. That quality is relevance. In a world that is experiencing unprecedented disruption, Jake takes us on a journey in the Holy Scriptures to help us see the relevance of biblical wisdom in today's world. He subtly guides us away from 'self-centre' to 'God-centre'. Helping us see the increasing need for collaborative thinking and action as it pertains to wealth-generation models.

I would consider the book a timely intervention for the church. To stop, think and review our approach of the concept of biblical prosperity.

May we be transformed into the image of the one who is the Author and Finisher of our faith as we read this book.

Imal Silva
Principal Partner
IS&P

ACKNOWLEDGMENTS

I acknowledge the unquantifiable investment in teaching and mentorship I have enjoyed under distinguished men of God who have taught me and still teach me in the way of the Lord.

Pastor Olubi Johnson - truly, instructors abound but fathers are few. You are a rare gem!

Dr. Lance Wallnau – your insight is truly profound. I thank God for blessing the body of Christ with you.

Olubamike Fadipe - thank you. Your insight and perspective is always fresh.

To my editor - thank you.

My family – you complete me.

DEDICATION

To the Body of Christ

INTRODUCTION

I grew up as one of four children brought up by a single parent. My mom was a high school teacher earning a meagre salary with which she catered for four children, some with special needs, and an aged mother. I knew what lack meant. Hand-me-downs were a thing of joy. Many years down the line, I am married and I have a son. My son, Jedidiah, was about two years old when my wife and I decided to take a break before our next conception. One day while we were sorting through some stuff he had outgrown with the intention to keep hand-me-downs to his prospective siblings, God spoke to me: "His siblings are out there naked and destitute. Do not keep anything until you are actually pregnant".

I spoke to my wife and we agreed to obey God. We gave out almost everything which still had value, which my son had outgrown. It took faith because that meant we will need to buy them again. The economics did not make sense. I began to ask God questions about wealth creation. I knew He must have a way to make His yoke easy because the Bible says His commandments are not burdensome. Some of the thoughts He has shared with me over the course of time are crystallized in this book.

It is my hope that all who read it will find a way or ways to multiply what God has put in their hands so that giving becomes a lifestyle and not a burden.

1

WEALTH: TODAY'S CONTEXT

Wealth is referred to as the abundance of valuable possessions or money; plentiful supply of a desirable thing from riches, substance, luxury, affluence, material possession. It can also describe abundance of values, character and valuable stuffs that someone possesses in copious measure.

Wealth is a variable and a relative term used to describe the size of valuable possessions from person to person, people to people, tribe to tribe, nation to nation and continent to continent. In a farm settlement, the farmer with the largest size of produce is perceived as the wealthiest, while the herdsman with the largest herd of cattle will be the richest in that regard. It might then be right to say that wealth has different genre. The world has a formal definition of wealth based on real value of wealth in assets and investments. There is a flipside to the world's informal definition of wealth with the unusual mode of assessing and describing wealth in bogus forms. The description of wealth here is based on perception of luxury, opulence and class this is deciphered from the style of living, the magnificence of mansion built, the opulence of the decor and stylish living, the number and type of luxury cars owned, the designer and fashionable outfits adorned, the jewellery diamonds, platinum and gold. This type of wealth would fall in the class of "make-believe" wealth.

Every year Forbes, a global media company, focusing on business, investing, technology, entrepreneurship, leadership and lifestyle declare the world's richest personality tagged World's Billionaires with chronicles of what they do, where they are from, and the value of their wealth and assets. These wealth are not described in local currency of the owners irrespective of their country of origin: not in Yen, Pounds, Euro, not even Naira, they are usually described in Billions of the global currency - Dollars.

Wealth is progressive in its nature, there was a time in not too far history that it was a big deal to be a Millionaire, today even million dollars are running out of fashion! I remember the first breakthrough I had in my mind demystifying earning a Million Naira in sales which is either to have a product of a Thousand Naira to sell to a thousand people or one of Fifty Thousand Naira to be bought by twenty people. This simplified idea helps to put wealth expectations in proper perspective giving details of factors and the interactions of factors. It also positions wealth creation as a journey.

The value of wealth is ranked across the globe and then stepped down to each continent and then to nations. The chronicles by Forbes are usually clear, not debatable and reckoned as a global truth, such that whoever is declared as World's richest or Billionaire by Forbes remain so until a richer Billionaire in total worth can oust the outgoing richest, so it is a continuous cycle of who has got more! It is believed that apart from the obvious expression of wealth, intensive actuarial and data analytics would have been done which will then be ranked to name the wealthiest, wealthier and the wealthy in the order of their financial wherewithal. Rankings are done based on continent, region, age range and gender reckoning.

Wealth for the Billionaire is not defined in terms of notes of currency or money! Not in cash at hand or cash in the bank! They are described on the basis of net worth - total value or worth of enterprise, assets and investments. For most individuals that Forbes analyses their wealth, many of them have assets, enterprise and investments with quite a number starting from nothing but benefited from a huge dose of discipline, energy, ideas, inspiration, leverage, opportunities, and zeal. Some of these billionaires have always been ambitious in a particular trade and career path; same earned them the Forbes list showing a level of consistency with the trade and career path that brought them to fame. Some of them had an unusual pattern of life as a youth. A few individuals are beneficiaries of inheritance from a privileged pedigree of great family wealth and a few benefitted from chance and opportunities. It is very likely that the substance of the inheritance would have been earned and gained by the progenitor of such families from a heavy dose of discipline, energy, ideas, inspiration, leverage, opportunities and zeal hoping the successive beneficiaries will have same abilities and capacity to sustain and manage such mass of wealth bequeathed and be able to transfer the same value of wealth if not more to generations thereafter. The implication of this is that such families must build "Empiredom Mind-set" in their family values.

The "Empiredom Mind-set" and "Wealth Creation Mind-set" are intangible characteristics and values that require consistency, grit and tenacity to ensure the flow through the lineage. This is certainly a tough call for many families and individuals. The ambition and desire to be wealthy starts with one person and might not be transferable. The British royal family guards their royal heritage jealously; they infuse, impute and nurture the royal lineage transferring class, culture, finesse, style and values in their offspring and generations thereafter. They start early for their generations with so much commitment and focus creating a closed environment for education, exposure and information.

It is noteworthy that there are common denominators to these wealthy individuals and "money bags". Apart from life principles that cut across most of them in terms of discipline, personality, drive, their wealth in assets and investments have been built by people at different levels: employees, customers, partners, team or advisory board offering countless number of jobs and varied goods and services across different categories.

Many have extravagant lifestyle with class, luxury and opulence being their brand and a penchant for bespoke and designer items which they flaunt for the world to see. On the other hand, some others live a simple life and many are engaged in philanthropy all over the globe.

As it stands, no generalized characteristics or features can be drawn across these wealthy generations. Each and every one of them from their diverse continents, nations, tribes, faith and values all live their lives differently, make their choices, pursue their dreams and ambitions walking their pathway. It ends up being a personal journey. One thing is certain and common; they are all on a personal journey even though they are usually in the eye of the public and some are regarded as celebrity or influencers. The tenure of their relevance in the class of the world's wealthy is not readily predictable especially in this era of disruptive innovations. Some reign on the journey for a while, some others fizzle out after a while losing their wealth position to another. Their relevance according to the ranking and rating is determined year in year out by external perception and independent data analysis and influenced by market forces, innovations, competition and many other factors.

2

WEALTH: GOD'S CONTEXT

"Beloved, I wish above all things that thou mayest prosper and be in health, even as thy soul prospereth"

3 John 1:2KJV

"Let them shout for joy, and be glad, that favour my righteous cause: yea, let them say continually, Let the LORD be magnified, which hath pleasure in the prosperity of his servant"

Ps.35:27KJV

"But thou shall remember the Lord thy God: for it is He that giveth thee power to get wealth that He may establish His covenant which He sware unto thy fathers, as it is this day".

The promise of God for His people to be wealthy is clear cut and must never be misunderstood! God has taken only one side and it is only for prosperity, great wealth and good success. The scriptures firmly articulate God's heartfelt cry for His people – "… that they may prosper". In all His promises generations after generations, He did not change His stance or opinion.

The reality, however, is that the church is in stark contrast to fulfilling this desire and promise. The church in this context refers to God's people, not a location or the institution. The concept of the church as a location and an institution has been deployed to milk the people of God. Funding the administrative and operational aspects of the Church as an institution and as a location in these last days has made false shepherds out of many men of God and has given rise to fleecing and milking the sheep without adequate feeding and nurturing.

"Son of man, prophesy against the shepherds of Israel, prophesy, and say unto them, thus saith the Lord GOD unto the shepherds; Woe be to the shepherds of Israel that do feed themselves! Should not the shepherds feed the flocks? Ye eat the fat, and ye clothe you with the wool, ye kill them that are fed: but ye feed not the flock. The diseased have ye not strengthened, neither have ye healed that which was sick, neither have ye bound up that which was broken, neither have ye brought again that which was driven away, neither have ye sought that which was lost; but with force and with cruelty have ye ruled them."

Ezek.34:2-4KJV

So we see a contrast between the church organization and the people who are supposed to be members or units of that church structure. Preachers live fat and enjoy celebrity status while the members struggle to stay afloat; many living in abject poverty. This is not God's design or desire. The closest of God's design and intention for the new testament church was described in the book of Acts where it is recorded that none was lacking in their midst.

"All the believers continued together in close fellowship and shared their belongings with one another. They would sell their property and possessions, and distribute the money among all, according to what each one needed."

Acts 2:44-45 (GNB)

This is how the church body was designed to function; being a strong covering for the weak, and helping the weak while the weak focus on developing strength!

"From whom the whole body fitly joined together and compacted by that which every joint supplieth, according to the effectual working in the measure of every part, maketh increase of the body unto the edifying of itself in love."

Eph. 4:16

Just like it is in the natural body, the fingers work in tandem not in isolation in order to lift a burden. This is God's design for how the burden of the curse of poverty is to be lifted off His people as they work in unison.

What constitutes poverty?

The World Bank defines a monetary threshold under which an individual is considered to be living in poverty by calculating the value of goods needed to sustain an adult and converting it into dollars. This value varies from country to country. In 2015, independent researchers working in collaboration with the World Bank updated the international poverty line to $1.90/day from the previous $1.25/day value set in 2008. According to 2018 report by The World Poverty Clock, Nigeria has overtaken India to become the poverty capital of the world with about 67% of her population living below the poverty line.

Poverty is labour and toil that is sufficient only to meet one's needs. If all that is left after paying tithe, tax and bills is just enough to meet needs until the next pay cheque comes; poverty beckons. This is a tough call and a cut above our standards or definition of poverty, but, this how God defines it.

"And unto Adam he said, Because thou hast hearkened unto the voice of thy wife, and hast eaten of the tree, of which I commanded thee, saying, Thou shalt not eat of it: cursed is the ground for thy sake; in sorrow shalt thou eat of it all the days of thy life; Thorns also and thistles shall it bring forth to thee; and thou shalt eat the herb of the field; In the sweat of thy face shalt thou eat bread,…"

Gen. 3:17-19

Many authors have defined wealth or financial freedom as the ability to continue living at your current standards without earning a work associated pay cheque for six (6) months or more. This is a life beyond the reach of the curse.

Before man's treason and fall which made God declare a curse upon the ground; man lived, fed and dwelt in abundance. Every fruit of the tree in the garden, except one, was meat for him. The trees were already in full blossom before Adam came. God made surplus provision for man to enjoy even before man was made. Adam's task was to keep and tend, that's all. It was the curse that brought the need for man to toil before he ate – his food and living comes out of his toil.

God's design for Adam is true for all man today. He desire that we enjoy in abundance and have an overflow.

"If you are willing and obedient, you shall eat the good of the land"

Isa. 1:19

Eat – not toil for or labour to produce. Which means 'good' is already in the land. God's desire is that His people become so stupendously rich that they lend to nations.

"Jehovah shall open to you His good treasure, the heaven to give the rain to your land in its season, and to bless all the work of your hand. And you shall loan to many nations, and you shall not borrow."

Deut. 28:12 (MKJV)

This promise of lending to nations is both corporate and individual. This means that what God wants for His children (each and every one) is a financial capacity that will enable them to lend to more than one nation - at least two nations. Talk about stupendous wealth! This is a task that is currently being undertaken by bodies such as United Nations Development Bank (UNDP), International Monetary Fund (IMF), the World Bank, and Paris Club among many others. Where is the 'Paris Club' for believers? Moslems have an Islamic bank which operates by providing interest-free loan facilities to its followers and customers but that principle (loan without interest) is biblical! Where are the Christian financial institutions that are lending to individuals, firms or corporate bodies at zero percent interest rate? Where is the fulfilment of God's promise? Is God's word not true?

Take a moment to put "lending to nations" into perspective. A Wikipedia article[1] showing the list of the top 10 countries with budgets exceeding $1trillion dollars, puts China at the top of the list with a budget in excess of $7 trillion and Italy at position 10, with a budget in excess of $1.1 trillion. For argument sake, let's say we pick the countries at the top and the bottom of the list as countries you aspire to lend to. That means we are talking about over $8 trillion. Can any individual or group provide financial service to such capacity? The Paris Club, an informal group of creditor nations whose objective is to find workable solutions to payment problems by debtor nations,[2] has so far since its existence signed agreements covering $538 billion dollars in debt to 90 countries.[3] As far as individual donations are concerned, Mr. Bill Gates tops the list with a whopping $28 billion so far given to charity and charitable causes.[4] Prince Al-Waheed bin Talal of Saudi Arabia has also been reported to pledge his $32 billion fortune to charity.[5] These charitable donations, noble and rare as they are, only amount to a drop in a bucket compared to what God has promised His people – "lending to nations". If we continue with this line of thought and speculate as to what will constitute a significant lending in a $7 trillion budget, what would you say? $1 trillion? According to a 2012 estimate[6] which ranks Islam as the second richest religion in the World with an estimate of $1.6 trillion in assets and puts the Roman Catholic Church at the top of the list with an untold amount in asset, maybe this church can lend to one nation but certainly not more. Yet, the scripture is definitely audacious in the promise – "lend to NATIONS". It would take a stupendous outpouring of wealth, the likes of which we still do not have terms to describe, to fulfil this promise.

"But as it is written, "Eye has not seen, nor ear heard," nor has it entered into the heart of man, "the things which God has prepared for those who love Him."

1 Cor. 2:9

What is the purpose of this stupendous outpouring of wealth? Is it to boast, gloat and indulge? Is it to oppress? No! I say again, No! God has no interest in petty-minded folks or empty barrels. Only those who have not found a purpose for their wealth take pleasure in pursuing lavish and often extravagant displays of what they possess.

"The LORD says, "The wise should not boast of their wisdom, nor the strong of their strength, nor the rich of their wealth."

Jer.9:23 (GNB)

This is the purpose of the wealth – to establish God's covenant.

"But thou shalt remember the LORD thy God: for it is he that giveth thee power to get wealth that he may establish his covenant which he sware unto thy fathers, as it is this day."

Deut. 8:18

The Scripture's first reference to the word - Covenant, is in relation to Noah and its import was the preservation of mankind.

"But with thee will I establish my covenant; and thou shalt come into the ark, thou, and thy sons, and thy wife, and thy sons' wives with thee."

Gen. 6:18

Therefore, God gives wealth to establish His covenant and He preserves life to establish His covenant. Hence, any wealth that does not have this as its primary focus - preservation of human lives is wealth wasted and God is checking to repossess and re-purpose such wealth in these last days.

"...because the abundance of the sea shall be turned unto thee, the wealth of the nations shall come unto thee"

Isa. 60:5 (RV)

The people who have the preservation of human lives as the purpose of their wealth will continue to be wealthy because God Himself will see to it. These people are operating Biblical principles and as long as God's word never fails, those principles will never fail.

Some of the principles they are operating, howbeit unknown to them are:

1) "What God the Father considers to be pure and genuine religion is this: to take care of orphans and widows in their suffering..."

Jas 1:27 (GNB)

No matter what your declaration of faith is, if it does not include taking care of the poor, weak and defenceless, you have excluded yourself from the outpouring of wealth that is coming.

2) "When you give to the poor, it is like lending to the LORD, and the LORD will pay you back."

Prov. 19:17(GNB)

Talk about an assured Return on Investment (ROI)! You become a creditor to God! Believe me, He does not default. He pays up what is due to you and extra at the appointed time. As the scripture says, it is good measure, pressed down, shaken together and running over.

According to biblical accounts, one of the wealthiest men that ever lived was King Solomon. He was so wealthy and his reign so prosperous that silver lost value. It was so abundant, it created a glut and market forces brought down its value.

"All King Solomon's drinking vessels were of gold, and all the vessels of the House of the Forest of Lebanon were of pure gold. None were of silver; silver was not considered as anything in the days of Solomon... 27 and the king made silver as common in Jerusalem as stone..."

1 Kings 10:21, 27

An article in MSN Money[7] puts the estimate, after an adjustment for inflation, at $2.2 trillion, making him the 5th wealthiest man of all time. This ranking puts Solomon behind Augustus Caesar and Genghis Khan who rank 4th and 1st respectively. One can only conjecture that his departure from God's statutes diminished his ability to amass wealth. Despite the ranking, Solomon was incredibly wealthy even by our modern day standards. The current title holder as the world's richest man (as at the time of this writing) is valued at a paltry $144 billion when compared to Solomon's $2.2 trillion. Yet the Bible boldly states "a greater than Solomon is here"

"The queen of the south shall rise up in the judgment with this generation, and shall condemn it: for she came from the uttermost parts of the earth to hear the Wisdom of Solomon; and, behold, a greater than Solomon is here."

Matt. 12:42

Was Christ bluffing or overstating His claims when He said "a greater than Solomon is here"? While on earth, did He live out the full expression of this abundance of wealth? To both questions the answer is No!

1) God is not a man that he should lie. He means what He said.

2) Christ did not live out the full expression of that abundance of wealth because He procured that right for us by His death, burial and resurrection. It was His redemptive work upon the cross that redeemed us from the curse. Until that redemptive work was done, the curse of the law including poverty held sway over all of mankind.

"Christ hath redeemed us from the curse of the law, being made a curse for us: for it is written, Cursed is every one that hangeth on a tree: 14 that the blessing of Abraham might come on the Gentiles through Jesus Christ..."

Gal. 3:13-14

However, we see snippets of His expression of wealth because:

(i) He had a treasurer (John 1:29). A pauper does not have a treasurer.

(ii) His purse was so rich that the treasurer stole frequently from the purse and the other disciples did not know (John12:6).

(iii) He fed multitudes, twice. This is one of the few miracles duplicated in His earthly ministry. To show us it was no fluke. Yes, He eventually fed both crowds by supernatural provision but His first question to His disciples about feeding the crowd is an indication of his financial capacity. His question was: "where can we find bread" not how much is it going to cost us?

It is said that if you call the Rolls Royce Company to ask for the cost of any of their cars, you will be told it means you cannot afford it. People who can afford it don't think or worry about the cost, they just get it. This is the same disposition we see here, "where can we find bread" not how much would it cost.

"When Jesus then lifted up his eyes, and saw a great company come unto him, he saith unto Philip, Whence shall we buy bread that these may eat?"

John 6:5

Philips' response also adds credence to the fact that there was a level of wealth on display in Christ's earthly ministry.

"Philip answered him, Two hundred pennyworth of bread is not sufficient for them, that every one of them may take a little."

John 6:7

Let's put the reply into perspective, a penny is the equivalent of a day's wage (Matthew 20:9). Hence, 200 penny worth of bread is equivalent to 200 days' wage. This was what was being considered as the budget for a meal to entertain guests! 200 days is like six (6) months. Pause and reflect, in your current financial standing, would you contemplate using the equivalent of six (6) months' pay cheque to entertain guests in one day?

This is Christ's pre-redemptive, conservative expression of wealth so that the full measure can be displayed in us, the church! Hallelujah! If six (6) months' pay cheque for lunch is the conservative outflow of God's plan for the abundance of wealth, what will be the full measure? 6 years earnings for dessert?

Break out of this mould of penury and lack; begin this journey and make demand on heaven and earth, for what God has in store for you is a deluge of wealth!

3

WHAT IS WEALTH?

Following the law of first mention, the book of Genesis, chapter 34 verse 29, is the first recorded use of the word wealth'. It was translated from the word 'chayil'' (H2428) – force, derived from the root word 'chiyl'' (H2342) which means to twist or twirl. The scholarly illustration of wealth will be to describe wealth as motion: a force that twists or twirls. The concept of twists implies bending and turning into a particular shape while twirl means to make something turn quickly in a circular motion. The interception of the twist and twirls motion connotes interplay of forces.

Never mind the illustration with basic physics which teaches that there are two opposing forces in action when an object is in a circular motion i.e. when it twists or twirls. These forces are (i) Centripetal and (ii) Centrifugal forces. According to the American Heritage Dictionary,[8] "the centripetal force is defined as the component of force acting on a body in curvilinear motion that is directed to the centre of curvature or axis of rotation while the Centrifugal force is defined as an apparent but equal opposing force drawing a rotating body away from the centre of rotation."

Wealth is a balance between these opposing forces vis-à-vis, the force that gathers (centripetal) and the force that scatters (centrifugal).

"There is that scattereth, and yet increaseth; and there is that withholdeth more than is meet, but it tendeth to poverty".

Prov. 11:24(KJV)

Wealth is a balance of forces: it causes a flow of energy from one direction to another and a return flow of energy from the opposite direction. Wealth runs like a complete cycle with resources flowing from one end to another and then back; the cycle continues. Real and true wealth is fluid; it flows with a multiplier effect.

Wealth is described more as the capacity for production, conversion and transfer of value that can be traded, invested, multiplied and expended. Wealth is hidden in exchanges, products, services and the in-between of these offers.

The simplicity of wealth is hidden in the arithmetic of multiplication as everything that results in wealth undergoes that process of a gain being multiplied by population i.e.

Wealth = Profit x Population

The value of anyone's wealth is measured by the profit or gain any product or service can generate with the multiplier effect of the number of people that can be aware, access, connect, identify, relate and patronize such products or services and as such, the more the merrier. The wealthy understand the power of numbers.

If one thousand people can pay Two Thousand Naira (N2,000) for a product or service, the revenue will be the sum of Two Million Naira (N2,000,000), now if the profit margin is 40%, then the total profit will be Eight Hundred Thousand Naira (N800,000). The world economy has experienced a high degree of disruption with the breakthrough of technology. Technology keeps demystifying the matrix of numbers and population, redefining the principles of gaining the numbers and population in offering products and services. Amazon's, billion dollar business is built on this principle.

4

WEALTH IS A CITY

"The rich man's wealth is his strong city"

Pro 10:15a

There is no force greater than the force of a community or a network or a team. Thomas J Stanley, in his research for the book "The Millionaire Next Door", said that all his millionaire respondents considered marriage a plus factor when it comes to accruing wealth. The scripture says one shall put a thousand to flight but two shall put ten thousand to flight. This implies an exponential increase in output by an addition of only one! Selah

"And the LORD said, Behold, the people is one, and they have all one language; and this they begin to do: and now nothing will be restrained from them, which they have imagined to do."

Gen. 11:6

Babel was the first city of reckon in the Bible started by a man called Nimrod who started building kingdoms; the Bible records that he began to build a mighty one on earth and Genesis 10:8-10 referred to him as a highly skilled hunter. Prior to Nimrod's kingdom building, no individual of all the generations had built any city, so Nimrod was a pioneer and a kingdom builder.

The Babel city started as an idea but it became a people dream: they were all of one brilliant idea and a defined objective which is to build a city whose top may reach heaven. There was a clear cut strategy of what needs to be done to build the city and what is required; make brick, burn them thoroughly for stone, use slime for mortar. There is no creative enterprise that is out of the reach of a people, network or team that is united in language and purpose.

"And the LORD said, Behold, the people is one, and they have all one language; and this they begin to do: and now nothing will be restrained from them, which they have imagined to do."

Gen. 11:6

This is God's testimony concerning the state of the people at the tower of Babel.

From the creation story, even the God-head exists as a team. In the creative process and conversations, God issued commands as He addressed nature and the unseen to bring forth that which is seen. At the climax of His creative process; God referred to Himself with a plural pronoun when He said "Let us make man..." (Genesis1:26).

One of the key indicators that every person focused on accumulating wealth should keenly note is the strength and value of all the relationships they have acquired and the ones they need to build. The relationships we have are a door on their own, as it opens us up to a world different from ours and the familiar. The relationships and intensity of relationships have the greatest impact on our livelihood. The relationship we have influences and defines us, gives us access to the competencies, depth, information, intelligence, knowledge, perspectives, resources, expertise and such that money cannot buy! The interaction of forces of personalities and the potentials therein remains one of the blessings of divinity. The potential of a good relationship is not only in a marriage relationship; good friendships, partnerships, and collaboration improves, polishes, multiplies and magnifies individual effort. Consider this: Microsoft built software applications, but the applications wouldn't have been of any use to anyone without connections and collaborations with computer system manufacturers, phone manufacturers and other devices whose product became a vehicle for Microsoft's products.

The greatest blessings of life and nature come from relationships - natural and supernatural. God often hides our breakthrough, deliverances, our miracles and the attainment of our highest dreams in relationships. Relationships offer courage, strength, leverage and platform. Leverage is the new currency of wealth and great success. The gap between where one is and where one needs to be can be fast-tracked through leverage which captures the wealth of resources and advantage available at one level and transmitted to a recipient moving step ahead of the ordinary.

The dynamics of relationship has twists and turns to its essence, sometimes with unpredictable and uninteresting acts and scenes, ups, downs, and curves charting a learning pathway. Joseph's life experience was a thriller with a rough childhood and unpleasant adulthood till it revealed that all the events, sights and sounds in his life were all part of a big salvation story and preservation of a race. Joseph could not have become the prime minister of Egypt without the tumultuous relationship he had with his brothers. If he was not implicated with Potiphar's wife, he was too smooth a lad; he couldn't have smelt the Pharaoh's palace as the divine encounter that brought him to limelight was crafted to take place in the prison. Joseph knew himself as a dreamer but the capacity to interpret dream was developed and honed right inside the palace when the opportunity came. Naaman would have lived and died a leper without the relationship he had with the slave girl in his house. Lot would have died in Sodom but for the apt intercession and unbeatable negotiation prowess of Abraham which was premised on kinship relationship.

A city is described many times by culture, landmark, location, history, resources and more importantly by the people. The description of a city is not enough without the description of the people and the essence of a people can never be enough without a description of who they are, where they come from and what they have in terms of resources.

"And the Lord God planted a garden eastward in Eden; and there he put the man whom he had formed. And out of the ground made the Lord God to grow every tree that is pleasant to the sight, and good for food; the tree of life also in the midst of the garden, and the tree of knowledge of good and evil. And a river went out of Eden to water the garden; and from thence it was parted, and became into four heads. The name of the first is Pishon: that is it which compasseth the whole land of Havilah, where there is gold; And the gold of that land is good: there is bdellium and the onyx stone. And the name of the second river is Gihon: the same is it that compasseth the whole land of Ethiopia. And the name of the third river is Hiddekel: that is it which goeth toward the east of Assyria. And the fourth river is Euphrates."

Genesis 2:8 - 14 (KJV)

The Bible describes Eden as a city: Eden was first described by the location - Eastwards, then by the man whom he had formed. Verse 10 describes other natural resources surrounding the city; River Pishon, Gold, Bdellium, Onyx, River

Gihon, River Hiddekel and River Euphrates. The description further detailed other landmarks such as Ethiopia and Assyria.

The wealth a city possesses is the cumulative wealth of her people; this wealth is usually a derivative of value having capacity of conversion from one form of resource to another; from natural resources to produced items, from a latent product to the household items. Nations are described by what they have, what they can produce and what they can offer other nations that are of value and same with cities. The nations that have so much value to offer others are ranked in their order of capacity to create value and their liberality to share the wealth of the value: nations like United States, United Kingdom and Asian nations remain the leading nations in terms of capacity to create value and the diversity of same. The United States and United Kingdom are liberal in sharing with nations who seemingly have lower capacity. The commitment of these big nations to respond to the world at large ranks them very high. That is why when there is conflict, epidemic, war or distress in any other nation; they are the first set to respond. Institutions in these nations also have same disposition. These commitments can be contested for their agenda or interests by diverse stakeholders, the context of these examples focus on action taken and response as they occur, not the analysis of intention or the politics that might be involved.

5

WEALTH IS AN ATTITUDE

"He that hath a bountiful eye shall be blessed; for he giveth of his bread to the poor."

Prov. 22:9

This is an interesting quote from the scriptures, wouldn't you say? This verse alludes that bounty is in the eye, just like beauty is in the eye of the beholder, meaning that a perception of abundance begins with the mind: eyes to capture abundance and disposition to curate it.

One of my mentors and teacher, Dr. Ralph Martin, defines wealth as anything you have that money cannot buy. Sadly, the world system has given us a whole new set of metrics for measuring wealth – money, money, money and all that money can buy. He shares his experience of over 40 years of driving but with only 2 events of a flat tire. In both instances, someone else pulled up and offered to change the tires for him! That might sound trivial – talk about wealth.

A friend of mine, born with the sickle cell haemoglobin, has lived almost 40 years without the compensatory Foetal haemoglobin that is seen in all HbS persons. His doctors could not understand how he had made it far. Let's do a bit of science to put this statement in perspective. Due to the abnormal S haemoglobin produced in sickle cell individuals, the body retains the foetal (baby) haemoglobin to help cope with stress in adult life. This does not occur in Haemoglobin A persons. However, in the case of my friend who is haemoglobin SS, his body did not retain or produce foetal haemoglobin for almost 40 years. Thus behaving like Haemoglobin A individual yet he had no complications associated with sickle cell disease. Now; that is wealth!

One of my favourite teachers on the subject of marketplace ministry, Dr. Lance Wallnau, defines wealth from another angle: he defines it as Assets, Access and Abilities. Hence, wealth is when your Chief Executive just takes a liking to you. Wealth is when the car dealer sells you your dream car at a giveaway price. Wealth is when your daughters prophesy and your sons are reputed as being wiser than Solomon. Wealth is when your son who is almost a teenager has never had to take a pill for a headache. Wealth is when there is a mudslide in your city and only your street was spared. Wealth is your natural ability to simplify the most difficult processes for your colleagues to understand. Wealth is simply being blessed! It is so much more than money and it begins with a positive and right attitude.

In pre-modern Israel, as recounted in the Old Testament, men of substance tallied their wealth in livestock. This was because the economy was agrarian and it was before the advent of money as a legal tender. However, I find it noteworthy to see the order of listing of the livestock these men possessed: sheep, camel, oxen, and asses.

"There was a man in the land of Uz, whose name was Job; and that man was perfect and upright, and one that feared God, and eschewed evil. And there were born unto him seven sons and three daughters. His substance also was seven thousand sheep, and three thousand camels, and five hundred yoke of oxen, and five hundred she asses, and a very great household"

Job 1:1-3

"And he entreated Abram well for her sake: and he had sheep, and oxen, and he asses, and menservants, and maidservants, and she asses, and camels."
Gen.12:16

I believe that God, knowing there would be only one compendium of scriptures, found a way to layer truths in each and every detail highlighted in the Bible. Like Apostle Paul rhetorically asked "Doth God care for oxen?" No, but for our sakes was it written. If it was not important or significant, it would not be included in the canon of scriptures. Men of old tallied their wealth in livestock: sheep which is a symbol of meekness, quietness, and submission, was listed first. I believe that this is to teach us that wealth is a downright positive and right attitude.

6

THE SNARE OF SALARY

"And the LORD God planted a garden eastward in Eden; and there he put the man whom he had formed. And out of the ground made the LORD God to grow every tree that is pleasant to the sight, and good for food; the tree of life also in the midst of the garden, and the tree of knowledge of good and evil. And a river went out of Eden to water the garden; and from thence it was parted, and became into four heads."

Gen. 2:8-10 (KJV)

This is God's design for watering the earth and providing sustained nourishment for her inhabitants: one river but four heads of streams. The names of the heads of streams are:

(i) Pishon (H6376) meaning spread or increase

(ii) Gihon (H1521) meaning bursting forth

(iii) Hiddekel or Tigris (H2313) meaning rapid

(iv) Euphrates (H6578) meaning fruitfulness

If you have ever worked for a wage, you can tell that there is nothing rapid about it; asides being static and highly predictable, what is rapid is the spending.

I acknowledge the work of Buddy Harrison in his book; Understanding God's Banking System, on this subject matter. He sheds great light on the rightful place a salary should hold in a believer's financial world.

The word 'Salary' is derived from the word, Salarium which comes from the Latin word Sol, meaning salt. In essence, salary is salt. The history of the word 'salary' dates back to the practice in the Roman empire of paying soldiers a weight of salt. This is the origin of the idiom "worth his salt". In many pre-modern cultures, salt was used as a seasoning and as a preservative. Useful as it may be, nobody sits down to eat a meal of salt. Just one teaspoonful can induce choking because it is a powerful desiccant. Salt overload can lead to electrolyte imbalance, arrhythmias, high blood pressure and ultimately death. No wonder people who subsist only on salary always suffer financial ill-health, transferred emotional distress due to not having enough. No matter how large the pay cheque coming in is, if it is the only stream flowing in your finances, trouble is brewing somewhere and it may come calling soon. Human needs are insatiable and unstable: the theory of consumption did not leave us in doubt on this. The Consumption theory by Keynes posits that consumption depends on disposable income which is the total amount of income available for use by individuals or household after tax and all deductions. The theory also clearly implies that increase in disposable income will directly impact on consumption.

You may say, "But I love my job. My pay cheque is just fine; my boss is a fair and just man" etc. No doubt about that. The point is that the wealth required to fulfil God's mandate cannot come from only one stream! It might be fun doing a little bit of arithmetic class: define or determine a value of wealth in desirable currency and figures that your mind can imagine for now… deduct your current consumption and costs from your income, then divide the proposed figure by your monthly disposable income; the figure will give you the number of months required to raise the desired figure of wealth.

"And God is able to make all grace abound toward you; that ye, always having all sufficiency in all things, may abound to every good work"

2 Cor. 9:8

"For we are his workmanship, created in Christ Jesus unto good works, which God hath before ordained that we should walk in them."

Eph. 2:10

It is true that good works doesn't save but they do say a lot about our Saviour, Jesus Christ. I once heard the story of an evangelist who went to share the Good news with the inhabitants of a remote location. One day while preaching in the streets, he preached to a little boy who asked him "Can your Jesus give me shoes?" As far as the boy was concerned, salvation begins with providing him with a pair of shoes. Thankfully, the preacher was able to give the boy a pair of shoes and then continued to win his soul for Christ. Take a moment to think about how many times you have shied away from doing a good work not because you did not desire to do it but because you did not have the power - means, resources or wealth to do it. You knew if you did that good work, it was going to mess with your finances and you were going to suffer for it. You knew to do well but you refrained from doing it! Of course with an excuse!

"Therefore to him that knoweth to do good, and doeth it not, to him it is sin"

Jas 4:17

This is the snare of the mono-economy of salary. Am I teaching an outright mutiny against gainful employment? No! On the contrary, there is a lot to learn from an employment – the discipline of time management, financial accounting, responsibility, submission, leadership, faithfulness, performance management, people management, teamwork, delegation, systems and structures building, organization and etc... If you have not been faithful in another man's who will give you your own? (Luke 16:12).

However, I am saying that God's first introduction of Himself to us was as a Creator (Genesis 1:1). Every believer must also aspire to create something: a product, a service, a venture, a book, a blog, some technology driven solution, an innovation, an art or artefact, some music, anything. This is wisdom: use the salary from your gainful employment rightfully, as what it truly is, Salt: either to flavour your meal or as a preservative while you are working out the details of what you intend to create. But by all means do not be complacent! Do not settle for Zoar! God has a bigger game plan in mind and He will not call a mediocre, who will be intimidated by wealth, to the kick-off.

7

THE CREATIVE PROCESS

Order

"In the beginning God created the heaven and the earth"

Gen. 1:1

I cannot overstate the fact that God, The Creator, created man to be a creator. God's first introduction of Himself to us is as "Creator". Hence, creating is innate to him. We return to the book of beginnings to decipher God's strategy for creating. The Genesis account of creation highlights steps in the creative process that we can learn from. The same steps were duplicated by the Lord Jesus in His miracle of feeding the multitudes. In both instances, we see that God's creative process begins with order.

"In the beginning God created the heavens and the earth. 2 And the earth was without form, and void; and darkness was upon the face of the deep. And the Spirit of God moved upon the face of the waters. 3 And God said, Let there be light: and there was light. 4 And God saw the light, that it was good: and God divided the light from the darkness."

Gen. 1:1-4

In the miracle of feeding the five thousand, the first instruction Christ gave was for the people to be seated in groups of 50 – ORDER!

"For they were about five thousand men. And he said to his disciples, Make them sit down by fifties in a company. [15] And they did so, and made them all sit down.[16] Then he took the five loaves and the two fishes, and looking up to heaven, he blessed them, and brake, and gave to the disciples to set before the multitude."

Lk 9:14

In the miracle of turning water to wine, the creative process also began with order.

"And there were set there six water pots of stone, after the manner of the purifying of the Jews, containing two or three firkins apiece. 7 Jesus saith unto them, Fill the waterpots with water. And they filled them up to the brim. 8 And he saith unto them, Draw out now, and bear unto the governor of the feast. And they bare it. 9 When the ruler of the feast had tasted the water that was made wine..."

John 2:6

The water pots were SET! Selah! Order is essential in creative processes. Whether in a remodelling (as seen in the Genesis account of creation), or in a multiplicative process (as seen in the miracle of the loaves), or in making something common special (as seen in the miracle of turning water to wine)

In the English language, there are only 26 alphabets yet there are millions of books, each unique in its own way, written with the same number of alphabets. How was this feat achieved? By ordering and re-ordering combinations of the 26 alphabets to make words that convey an idea. For example, ABLE and ABEL are made up of the same alphabets but they do not mean the same thing neither do they convey the same idea. What is the difference? – Order! Imagine that the letters of the word ABLE were not definitely set in order and they were kind of floating around. Wouldn't that define a medical condition known as Dyslexia? Hence, it is not only important to have the right letters but having them in an ordered or structured format makes the difference between sense and nonsense. One of the ways to begin creating wealth is to find something that exists and to reorder it to be more efficient, more cost effective, more accessible, better adapted and so on. There is no limit to what you can achieve with a little bit of order. Retail markets existed before big names like Walmart, AliExpress or Amazon but these mega corporations have carved a niche for themselves by ordering a process we are all very familiar with to become more efficient.

Division

"And God saw the light, that it was good: and God divided the light from the darkness. 5 And God called the light Day, and the darkness he called Night. And the evening and the morning were the first day. 6 And God said, Let there be a firmament in the midst of the waters, and let it divide the waters from the waters. 7 And God made the firmament, and divided the waters which were under the firmament from the waters which were above the firmament: and it was so. 8 And God called the firmament Heaven. And the evening and the morning were the second day. "

Gen. 1:4 – 8

Again, we return to the book of beginnings to see the role division plays in the creative processes. This concept is a bit contrary to the logic taught by the world. Think back to your education in elementary arithmetic, you were taught that division makes things smaller. Say for example, you divide 8 by 2, the result is 4 not 10 and the sum of the parts add up to the whole, 8 not 12. However, we see another law of division at work in God's creative processes: God divides and the sum of the parts is greater than the whole. God divided light from darkness and the sum of the two parts produced an entirely new phenomenon called Day!

In the miracle of turning water to wine, as recorded in the account of John's gospel, Jesus ordered the servants to divide the water from the cup, from the water in the pots and it became wine.

"And he saith unto them, Draw out now, and bear unto the governor of the feast. And they bare it. 9 When the ruler of the feast had tasted the water that was made wine..."

John 2:8

In the miracle of the loaves, the Lord Jesus multiplied the little boy's lunch by dividing it and it fed 5,000 men not counting women and children. If we speculate, a wife and child for every man present, we are talking about 15,000 people, maybe more. Division was one of the keys of this particular miracle.

"Then he took the five loaves and the two fishes, and looking up to heaven, he blessed them, and brake, and gave to the disciples to set before the multitude"

Lk 9:16

And in the story of the wife of the sons of the prophets who came to Elisha begging for money to pay her creditors - 2 Kings 4; the prophet instructed her to use what she already has which is the jar of oil. She got more jars of oil and started pouring out, she started unleashing and as she divided the jar of oil, the multiplier effect came upon the oil and it flowed till she got to the last jar and then the oil ceased. It is absolutely certain that if she had more capacity and more jars, the oil would have kept flowing.

In nature, we see that the process of embryogenesis which is the process by which the embryo forms and develops is driven by series of divisions. It starts with the fertilization of the ovum by the sperm. Once fertilized, the ovum is referred to as a zygote. The zygote undergoes mitotic divisions with no significant growth leading to the development of a multicellular embryo. Cell division producing a cluster of cells that is the same size as the original zygote is called cleavage. After the 7th cleavage has produced 128 cells, the embryo is called a blastula[9]. A series of complex processes including somitogenesis and organogenesis advances embryo growth until gestation is complete and the baby is born. After birth, division continues in the cells of the skin, bone marrow and many parts of the body and that is what we call growth.

Today, many countries of the world rely on the energy generated from a nuclear reactor to meet power, lighting and heating needs of their societies. The science behind the power generation of a nuclear reactor is nuclear fission. Nuclear fission is the subdivision of a heavy atomic nucleus, such as that of uranium or plutonium into two fragments of roughly equal mass. The process is accompanied by the release of a large amount of energy, radioactive products are formed and several neutrons are emitted. These neutrons can induce fission in a nearby nucleus of a fissionable material that can repeat the sequence, causing a chain reaction[10] the sequence is fission – energy + nuclear emission – fission.

Division, as taught by the world leads to reduction. But God uses multiplicative divisions to advance His creative process. His wisdom is a division leading to increase such that the sum of the parts is greater than the whole. An irony? That is our God! He is the mega-supernova who hides Himself in a black hole (2 Sam. 22: 7-14; 1 Jn 1:5).

The Garden of Eden was watered by two sources: a mist that rose to water the earth and a stream that parted into four heads. No matter how meagre your stream of income is, you must part it into savings, investment, basic needs and alms. You should work out what ratios to use but remember the injunction to save before you spend and not afterwards. Your savings can be used to acquire assets, kick off a business or used to cushion the effect of an economic recession. Your investments should be immediate but lightweight: stocks, bonds, treasury bills, etc. Make provision to incur some loses and do not be caught in the lie of get-rich-quick schemes.

I lost some money myself in the cryptocurrency rave of 2017 – 2018 as well as in the Ponzi scheme of www.chain.group. However, I was able to cushion the effect with revenue from other sources. Sadly, I know colleagues who went a-borrowing and eventually lost thousands of dollars to the MMM scheme because they wanted a quick fix. Some of them are still paying to offset debt incurred from the loss.

Gathering

"And God said, Let the waters under the heaven be gathered together unto one place, and let the dry land appear: and it was so. 10 And God called the dry land Earth; and the gathering together of the waters called He Seas: and God saw that it was good."

Gen. 1:9

Once again, we turn to the account of the beginnings to see another of God's creative processes. After He had ordered, and divided; He gathered. Two new things appeared when God gathered the waters: the earth and the sea. From these 'products of gathering', God called forth the springing of new things: birds and fishes from the sea; trees and herbs from the earth.

"And God said, Let the earth bring forth grass, the herb yielding seed, and the fruit tree yielding fruit after his kind, whose seed is in itself, upon the earth: and it was so. 20 And God said, Let the waters bring forth abundantly the moving creature that hath life, and fowl that may fly above the earth in the open firmament of heaven. 21 And God created great whales, and every living creature that moveth, which the waters brought forth abundantly, after their kind, and every winged fowl after his kind: and God saw that it was good."

Gen.1:11 - 21

Hence, gathering not only produces new things, it also produces raw materials for the creation of other things. What creative processes are you currently undertaking? Is it a product or service? What is the end-product, by-product or waste product? What more can be done with what you have produced? Can it become raw material for another creative venture?

Contrast a single-celled bacteria to man, and you will see the complexity and sophistication of man's body which is a far cry from the simplicity seen in those lower organisms. In man, an aggregation of cells make a tissue, a collection of tissues make an organ and a gathering of organs make a system and diverse systems of the body make a whole man.

According to the online English dictionary, Wiktionary, [11] "Gather" means to:

a. Collect things that are normally separate

b. Harvest food

c. Accumulate over time, to amass little by little

d. Congregate or assemble

e. Grow gradually larger by accretion

f. Bring parts of a whole closer

g. Haul in; to take up

h. Infer or conclude; to know from a different source

Gathering is an important step in any creative process because it often caps the process and helps prevent wastage. Whatever is not gathered goes to waste.

"When they were filled, he said unto his disciples, Gather up the fragments that remain, that nothing be lost. 13 Therefore they gathered them together, and filled twelve baskets with the fragments of the five barley loaves, which remained over and above unto them that had eaten."

John 6:12

In this account of the feeding of five thousand, the need had been superlatively met by God's instantaneous, creative processes of ordering and dividing, working through Jesus Christ. Yet, Christ was still focused on preventing wastage, therefore, He asked his disciples to gather up the fragments. Talk about a lean management system! Indeed, God is the author of all lean processes. Much more than the meagre meal of five loaves of bread and two fishes which was started with, twelve baskets full were gathered.

Ever wondered what Christ did with those twelve baskets of fragments? Knowing the character of God, I surmise that those fragments probably were used to reward the boy who offered his meal and to meet the need of some other people. When we fail to gather, we promote wastage and fail to reward the system that produced the initial result. The consequence is a break in the cycle of creation.

Nigeria is a classic but sad example of a nation that failed to collate, collect or amass revenue that could have been generated from the natural gas reserve that sits upon her vast oil wells. According to the Nigeria National Petroleum Corporation, the nation lost $710 million to gas flaring in 2016.[12] A country with one of the 10 largest natural gas reserves in the world, Nigeria flares 17.2 billion cubic metres of gas yearly.[13] This is equivalent to one quarter of the current power consumption of the entire African continent.[14] As at 2002, one of the oil companies operating in the Niger-Delta region of Nigeria had been estimated to have been flaring gas for 30 years.[15] Adjusting for inflation, fluctuations in the exchange rate, variation in tenure of exploration of different companies and the gas reserves available at various oil wells; collectively, Nigeria may have lost in excess of $1 trillion to gas flaring over a 30 year period. Such monumental loss could have been prevented and the revenue used to reward inhabitants of the oil- rich region or further other causes in the nation. This may have prevented the militancy and agitations to secede that are plaguing the nation. I still wonder why these losses are captured shamelessly without any investment towards revamping the flared gas and the colossal loss.

"Now therefore let Pharaoh look for a man who is discreet and wise, and set him over the land of Egypt. ³⁴ Let Pharaoh act, and let him appoint officers over the land, and take up the fifth part of the land of Egypt in the seven plenteous years. ³⁵ And let them gather all the food of those good years that come, and lay up grain under the hand of Pharaoh, and let them keep food in the cities."

Gen. 41:33

In the biblical account of the world's first global economic recession, the recession was so severe that the people gave their gold, cattle, land and themselves over to the government in exchange for grain. Citizens of foreign lands also brought their wealth, of their own volition to the government that had sense enough to listen to the wisdom of gathering. Egypt thrived and rose to worldwide prominence because God gave Joseph the wisdom to gather the increase of the land. Imagine that Pharaoh did not heed the wisdom of God through Joseph, to gather the increase of the years of plenty. Certainly, he, his household, all Egyptians and all the citizens of the then known world would have perished. Would God have been liable? No! Would God have fulfilled His promise of 7 years of plenty? Definitely! However, the foreknowledge of events and the prosperity preceding the famine would not have profited them if they didn't apply the wisdom of gathering.

I believe everybody experiences change in seasons at some point in life: years of abundance followed by a season of drought. The abundance could be in productive relationships, mentorship, finances, knowledge, opportunities, information, businesses etc. If you are in that season now, begin to ask the Lord for wisdom on how to gather the abundance. If you are currently experiencing a drought, were you faithful in gathering?

"Now there cried a certain woman of the wives of the sons of the prophets unto Elisha, saying, Thy servant my husband is dead; and thou knowest that thy servant did fear the LORD: and the creditor is come to take unto him my two sons to be bondmen. 2 And Elisha said unto her, What shall I do for thee? tell me, what hast thou in the house? And she said, Thine handmaid hath not anything in the house, save a pot of oil. 3 Then he said, Go, borrow thee vessels abroad of all thy neighbours, even empty vessels; borrow not a few. 4 And when thou art come in, thou shalt shut the door upon thee and upon thy sons, and shalt pour out into all those vessels, and thou shalt set aside that which is full. 5 So she went from him, and shut the door upon her and upon her sons, who brought the vessels to her; and she poured out. 6 And it came to pass, when the vessels were full, that she said unto her son, Bring me yet a vessel. And he said unto her, There is not a vessel more. And the oil stayed."

2 Kings 4:1 - 6

This account tells the story of a widow, the wife of one of the sons of the prophet, whose husband left a debt behind when he died. As the story goes, her wealth creation capability ended when she had no more vessels available from that which she had gathered.

Contemporary examples exist of corporations whose sole business and wealth relies on gathering. Facebook, AirBnB, AliBaba, and Uber are examples of mega corporations that have become a force to reckon with in the global economy just by applying the principle of gathering. Facebook, for example, is the largest owner of media content in the world, yet it has no TV show, no magazine in print, no photo gallery, no art museum; nothing. What Facebook has done is provide a service that gathers media content from individuals (willing subscribers) throughout the world. AirBnB owns no piece of real estate, yet it is the biggest owner of real estate in the world. Its success relies on gathering real estate properties from owners around the world. Same goes for the retail giant Amazon, AliBaba, and the taxi corporation - Uber. Certainly, these services (transportation, retail, property management etc.) had existed before such big names but these companies found a way to carve a niche for themselves in the industry by gathering services or products.

The biggest example of the force of gathering in our Solar System is the Sun. Being at the centre of our solar system; it is almost like a deafening cry given to us by God through nature to attest to the remarkable power that is made available when we deploy the wisdom of gathering. The sun is by far the most important energy source for life on earth[15]. It provides light, heat, magnetism and a measure of time. The sun's average luminance is about 1.88 Giga candela per square metre, its surface temperature is about 5,505 degrees celsius[16] and its magnetic field varies across its surface from 1–3,000 gauss.[17] The energy of the sunlight supports almost all life on earth by photosynthesis and drives earth climate and weather. At its core, the sun's energy production apparatus is driven by a series of steps called the Proton- Proton chain that converts Hydrogen to Helium in what is known as Nuclear Fusion.[18] Four free protons of Hydrogen are fused into a single alpha particle of Helium nucleus with the concomitant release of energy at the mass-energy conversion rate of 4.26 million metric tons per second.[19] This is equivalent to the energy released when 9.192 x 1010 megatons of explosive is set off per second.

A tremendous amount of power is made available when we gather (Eph. 3:20) and in that state of being gathered or unity, God has commanded the blessing of Life (Ps 133: 1-3)

.

AUTOMATE

"We who believe, then, do receive that rest which God promised. It is just as he said, "I was angry and made a solemn promise: 'They will never enter the land where I would have given them rest!' "He said this even though his work had been finished from the time he created the world. [4] For somewhere in the Scriptures this is said about the seventh day: "God rested on the seventh day from all his work."

Heb. 4:3 (GNB)

Amazing verse of scripture! God finished all His works from the time He created the earth and from that time till now, He is resting. This means that God is no longer (actively) involved in the day to day running of the Earth. He is not somewhere flaming the sun to come on to show the rising of each day or turning the wheels of the earth to ensure that the earth keeps rotating or herding the four winds of the earth like a sheep herd to ensure the constant supply of air. Man's contraption of idols and demons called gods may perform such mundane tasks but

Jehovah is much too wiser and bigger for that! His wisdom, as evident in nature, is the wisdom to automate.

Our history of automation dates back to 1946 when the term was coined in the automobile industry to describe the increased use of automatic device in production lines. It is defined as a technology concerned with performing a process by means of programmed commands resulting in a system that operates with minimal or no human intervention.[20] If man can do this, how much more the Almighty! Examine any process of nature and you will see God's automation set up in it. The Water Cycle, Oxygen Cycle, Kreb's Cycle, etc. even life has its own cycle. Therefore, after you have done all the ordering, dividing, and gathering required of wealth creation, remember to automate so that you may find rest.

This truth is the intersection at which many rich people fail. They work hard at other things but fail to automate so they find no rest and the wealth they have accumulated does not perpetuate beyond them. However, a small number of wealthy people have learnt what it means to automate a wealth creation system. According to Forbes compendium of "America's Richest Families" published in 2015, the Walton Family, owners of Wal-Mart, is arguably the richest family in the world with an estimated asset of $149 billion.[21] The Rothschild family might be the wealthiest but with an untold amount in asset; the title goes to the Waltons, for now. Walmart is an American multinational retailing corporation that operates as a chain of hypermarkets, discount department stores and grocery stores. It was founded in 1962 by Sam Walton.[22] As of January 2017, Walmart has 11, 695 stores and clubs operational in 68 countries under 63 banner[23] and according to the Fortune Global 500 tally of 2016, it is the world's largest company by revenue.[24] Now, that is an example of what it means to be a prodigious accumulator of wealth by automating a wealth creation system outliving the founder.

In order to automate, you must find the wisdom that will connect the waste product or by-product of one process to the raw material of a new process. If it still requires your presence or significant involvement to run, you have not yet automated the process. The wisdom of automation sets multiplication in motion, gives room for growth, expansion, sporadic increase and of course rest!

Amazon as a global online store; does not need Jeff Bezos to attend to every sale made or to respond to all enquiries and resolve any issue regarding purchase, refund or customers dissatisfaction; everything runs itself on applications, systems and a few human intervention.

8

POWER

"But thou shalt remember the LORD thy God: for it is he that giveth thee power to get wealth that he may establish his covenant which he sware unto thy fathers, as it is this day."

Deut. 8:18

"Where no oxen are, the crib is clean: but much increase is by the strength of the ox."

Prov. 14:4

"A gracious woman retaineth honour: and strong men retain riches."

Prov. 11:16

These scriptures provide grounds for this chapter on power. It takes power to get wealth, power to increase wealth and power to retain it. None of the strategies we discussed in preceding chapters will be possible without sufficient input of power.

Both words 'Power' and 'strength' as quoted above are translated from the Hebrew word 'Koach' (H3581) which means firm, vigour, force, capacity, and large lizard (chameleon). I acknowledge the teaching of Dr. Lance Wallnau on this. It was he who first exegete this scripture to me.

Hence, these verses of scripture can be read as "...much increase is by the chameleon-like ability of the ox" and "...it is he that giveth thee chameleon-like ability to get wealth..."

What in the world does a chameleon know about getting wealth? What abilities of the chameleon uniquely apply to creating and amassing wealth? For many, stealth or camouflage is the first thing that comes to mind in association with the word, chameleon. However, not all species of chameleons are able to change the colour of their skin in order to camouflage into their surroundings.[25]

Here is a list of amazing cool facts about a chameleon: [26]

1. Chameleons can camouflage. Not all species though

2. Chameleon eyes have 360 degree arc vision and can look in both directions at once

3. They vary in size and structure

4. They have a ballistic tongue that is 1.5 – 2 times the length of their bodies

5. Male chameleons are usually ornamented with horn-like projections.

6. They can't hear much

7. Chameleons can see in both visible and ultraviolet light spectrum

8. They are omnivores

The aforementioned are the abilities of a chameleon. We will see how these relate to wealth creation and accumulation.

This approach, to learn about wealth creation strategies from a chameleon is not novel or unscriptural. Indeed, the book of Proverbs teaches wisdom from the life and habits of four creatures that are exceedingly wise.

"There be four things which are little upon the earth, but they are exceeding wise: [25] The ants are a people not strong, yet they prepare their meat in the summer; [26] The conies are but a feeble folk, yet make they their houses in the rocks; [27] The locusts have no king, yet go they forth all of them by bands; [28] The spider taketh hold with her hands, and is in kings' palaces"

Prov. 30:24 - 28

What can we learn from the chameleon?

Camouflage

This is an important survival ability that allows the chameleon to avoid predator and to creep upon its prey. The chameleon does this by rearranging the cells in its skin which contains a lattice of guanine nanocrystals that interact with light rays to reflect the wavelength of colours of choice. Thus the chameleon can take on the colour of its environment and switch on its stealth mode.[27]

Everyone who desires to create or accumulate wealth must know, learn and practice his or her stealth mode. Dr. Strive Masiyiwa, the CEO of Econet group, teaches a series on leadership and business via Facebook and in one of his posts, he shares a story of how a bunch of guys inadvertently sold out their company's high profile bid by uncanny chatting.[28] These guys had no stealth in their business venture and some other guy, who overheard their conversation, took the business from right under them. Wealth creation requires a certain amount of stealth. I recommend that you follow Dr. Strive Masiyiwa on Facebook. His insights on the African marketplace are invaluable.

Even the Lord Jesus, who is the fullness of the Godhead bodily, came to earth in stealth mode. The scripture says if the princes of this world had known, they would not have crucified the Lord of glory. They didn't know what He came to accomplish because He came in stealth mode. He was not braggadocios. His birth, training, commissioning into ministry, the purpose of His death and resurrection, were all wrapped in a mystery yet it was all in plain sight. He could have chosen the palace but He was born in a manger, yet a horde of angels heralded his birth. His baptism was public yet His endorsement by the Father, which happened in the same event, was private: only John heard the voice. His commissioning into ministry was not done by the High Priest at a glamorous celebration in the temple at Jerusalem; No! It was at an obscure wedding party that was poorly funded and poorly organized. What sort of wedding party runs out of wine; and a cheap wine at that? Amazingly, this was where and how God chose to commission Jesus into ministry. Who would have thought that Jesus' death, something that has completely and eternally changed the course of human existence, would happen on an obscure hill in the outskirts of a city like Jerusalem? Everything was all wrapped up in unprecedented events and seeming coincidences. That is camouflage; that is stealth! If God were to act like you and I, He would have delayed the sacrificial death of His Son until the 21st century when technology would have afforded Him a billion hits on YouTube and everyone will be able to see Him display meekness even in the face of death. His words would have become quotes. I am certain that videos of such gory sights of his crucifixion would have gone viral and gain so much sympathy. More so, after His resurrection, His following on Instagram would have been in billions. Pictures of Him walking through walls, breaking bread with his disciples on the road to Emmaus, His ascension etc. would be buzzing on Snapchat. His Facebook account would have gone from private to 'public figure'! Rather, God chose to act in stealth mode so that the wealth of conversion may follow those who truly believe.

This is the admonition of the Holy Spirit to us all:

"Let this mind be in you, which was also in Christ Jesus: ⁶ Who, being in the form of God, thought it not robbery to be equal with God: ⁷ But made himself of no reputation, and took upon him the form of a servant, and was made in the likeness of men: ⁸ And being found in fashion as a man, he humbled himself, and became obedient unto death, even the death of the cross. ⁹ Wherefore God also hath highly exalted him, and given him a name which is above every name: ¹⁰ That at the name of Jesus every knee should bow, of things in heaven, and things in earth, and things under the earth; ¹¹ And that every tongue should confess that Jesus Christ is Lord, to the glory of God the Father."

Phil. 2:5 - 10

Be comfortable being a man of 'no reputation'. Let your reputation be your integrity, character, chivalry, finesse, kindness, and wisdom. Don't keep a reputation of what you wear, where you live, how you travel, where you eat or any such mundane and vain externals. Here is my recommendation: Don't go broke trying to look rich. Let your Sunday best be a fraction of your worth in assets. Live below your means. Adopt, develop and practice stealth mode. What is stealth mode to you might not be stealth mode to me. So, find out what defines stealth or camouflage for you and stick with it.

To turn on its stealth mode, the chameleon changes the arrangement of the guanine crystals in its skin. In essence, for the camouflage to hold as the chameleon moves and changes scene, it must keep rearranging its skin crystals. The true wealth creator must be one suitably adapted to the process of learning, unlearning and relearning. This is true education!

Omnivores

Chameleons have a very wide range of diets including insects, other lizards, young birds, snails, worms, banana, tomatoes, lettuce, oats and other plant sources of food.[29] Similarly, for a wealth creator and accumulator, no legal and legitimate venture should be off the menu. From bonds and stocks to investment in blue chip companies and start-ups, to real estate to financial services and consulting, all must be in your purview. You must be ready to start multiple concerns, merge with and/or acquire other smaller companies when the need arises. The richest man in Africa, Aliko Dangote, is an example of an omnivorous accumulator of wealth. According to Forbes, he ranks 67th on the world's list of billionaires and is valued at $12.5 billion.[30] His company, The Dangote Group, has interest in everyday commodities e.g. sugar, salt, pasta, cement, as well as transportation, oil and gas, banking, manufacturing, telecommunication, agriculture, and had previously expressed interest in buying the English Premier League club - Arsenal.

The classification, omnivore, was traditionally premised on the behaviour of both plant and animal tissue in diet.[31] With more technological advancement however, this classification has been conditioned into two context specific definitions: Behavioural and Physiological. Behavioural classification refers to the habit of actively consuming plant and animal materials while the physiological classification refers to the adaptation to derive energy and nutrient from both animal and vegetation.[32] No matter how much a cow craves meat, it cannot eat meat because it does not have the physiological adaptation to process meat. But omnivores, equipped with canine, incisor, molars and premolars are empowered to cut, tear, chew and grind anything and everything on the menu.

Teeth

"Arise, O LORD; save me, O my God: for thou hast smitten all mine enemies upon the cheek bone; thou hast broken the teeth of the ungodly."

Ps 3:7

The Hebrew word translated to teeth in this text is 'shen' (H8127) which is from the primitive root, shaman (H8150) which means to point, pierce, whet, sharpen, teach diligently. It takes growth and practice to become a well-adapted omnivore.

"And when he came unto Lehi, the Philistines shouted against him: and the Spirit of the LORD came mightily upon him, and the cords that were upon his arms became as flax that was burnt with fire, and his bands loosed from off his hands. 15 And he found a new jawbone of an ass, and put forth his hand, and took it, and slew a thousand men therewith."

Judg. 15:14-15

Samson, under the unction of the Spirit of the Lord killed a thousand men with the jawbone of a donkey. An impossible task by any standard! But the Holy Spirit superimposing upon a well-honed skill can accomplish the impossible. As we see in the example of Bezaleel who was contracted in the building of the Temple or as seen in the example of the first deacons appointed in the service of tables in the early church – they were men full of faith and the Holy Ghost.

Digestion

For some omnivores, e.g. Man, digestion begins in the mouth by the incorporation of carbohydrate digesting enzymes in the saliva. This is in contrast to carnivores that begin their digestive processes in the stomach. Carnivores bite off and swallow large chunks of meal (essentially meat) without much processing in the mouth. This is to avoid the degradation of its own body parts by proteolytic enzymes which will be required to digest protein based meals. The wealth omnivore must therefore, be able to begin 'digestion' – processing, breakdown, and assimilation of business opportunities upon first contact or sight.

The story is often told of the famous (or otherwise infamous) meeting between Napoleon Hill and Andrew Carnegie, then the richest man in the world. It was purported that in that meeting, Andrew Carnegie gave Napoleon Hill the opportunity of a lifetime: to research, discover and publicize the secret of success by interviewing the (then known) richest men in the world. Napoleon Hill was to undertake this task for one year without pay or a promise of reward. The interesting part, which bears reference to the point being made here, is that the offer was valid only for a few minutes. Andrew Carnegie did not give Napoleon Hill the opportunity to take a few days to count the cost. Hill was to respond in that instant whether he was willing to take up the offer or not. The rest as they say is history. Napoleon Hill went on to publish the widely successful book "Think and Grow Rich".

Sometimes, great opportunity presents itself in the most bizarre and unlikely way. David's opportunity for proximity to his place of destiny presented itself as a duel with a giant. Jacob's transformation into a 'Prince with God' was packed as a wrestling bout with an unknown assailant. Abraham's promise of a son was hidden in a midday picnic with strangers. The Shunamite got her miracle and access to the miraculous when she offered Elijah a bed and a meal. The true wealth omnivore must be able to identify, process and absorb opportunity the instant it presents itself no matter how bizarre or unlikely it looks and they must be able to take the risk.

Ornamented

Male chameleons have a horn-like projection. The first mention of the word 'horn' in the Bible is Exodus 21. The word 'Horn' appears 36 times in 34 verses of the Bible. . It is translated from the Hebrew words naggach (H5056) which means 'to butt', nagach (H5055) which means to war against, gore; qaran (H7160) to push; qeren (H7161) – by implication a flask, a corner of the altar, a peak, a ray of light, power. To push is to Pray Until Something Happens (corner of the altar, power), Persevere Until Something Happens (a peak), to stick with the Process Until something Happens.

"A gracious woman retaineth honour: and strong men retain riches."

Prov. 11:16

Wealth creation and accumulation requires a degree of fierceness and tenacity. It is not for weak hearted folk.

In the last century or so of man's history, billions of dollar and millions of man-hour have gone into research to uncover the key to success. At first, researchers thought it was intelligent quotient, a few years later research shifted and emotional intelligence was the new pill for success. However, a recent research conducted by pioneering psychologist and author, Angela Duckworth, has revealed that success has only one key – GRIT![33] Many studies have been carried out on grit or grittiness, bringing it to limelight as an important success factor. Several years before now, focus was high on the varied spectrum of intelligence and brilliance. Recently researchers are unearthing the fact that being successful in life is much more than knowledge, ability to learn quickly and easily, rather one characteristic emerged as significant predictor of success and that was GRIT. It was described with words like passion, perseverance for long term goals, stamina, sticking with the present and the future for years, living life like a marathon. This was Angela Lee Duckworth's submission in her TED Talks Education.

Duckworth defines GRIT as passion plus persistence. As defined by the English dictionary, GRIT is strength of mind; great courage or fearlessness, fortitude. It can also be defined as the determination or doggedness required to start and satisfactorily complete a given task.

As I write this, a scene from the movie "Men of Honour"[34] starring Cuba Gooding Jr. and Robert DeNiro comes to mind. The movie is the depiction of the life of Carl Brashear a Navy Diver Cadet who suffered undue hardship under the command of an officer who was a white supremacist; played by Robert DeNiro. Carl Brashear, played by Cuba Gooding Jr., and other trainees were given a task to find, assemble and retrieve a flange of equipment under water. The only measure of success was the completion of the task; time was not an issue. In spite of the freezing temperature of the water and sabotage by his commanding officer, Carl went on to complete the task in 9 hours, 31 minutes in contrast to 1 hour 37 minutes recorded by the first Cadet to complete the task. What kept him going for 8 extra hours? Grit!

Admiral William H. McRaven once said, "If you want to change the world, wake up daily and lay your bed". The wisdom in this profound statement is that the grittiness or persistence required to complete mundane, quotidian tasks, is the same grittiness required to change the world. In his book "Outliers", Malcolm Gladwell touched briefly on this subject matter in the chapter: "Rice paddies and Maths". He described how rice farmers who invested the extra hour before dawn to tend their paddies usually came out with a better harvest. He drew a parallel between this and the performance of Asian students in mathematics. According to him, the key was not in the genetics or diet; it was in staying with it for longer. In other words, GRITTINESS!

This nascent discovery of grittiness as the key to success has long been revealed in the Word.

"Be strong and of a good courage: for unto this people shalt thou divide for an inheritance the land, which I sware unto their fathers to give them. [7] Only be thou strong and very courageous, that thou mayest observe to do according to all the law, which Moses my servant commanded thee: turn not from it to the right hand or to the left, that thou mayest prosper whithersoever thou goest. [8] This book of the law shall not depart out of thy mouth; but thou shalt meditate therein day and night, that thou mayest observe to do according to all that is written therein: for then thou shalt make thy way prosperous, and then thou shalt have good success. [9]

Have not I commanded thee? Be strong and of a good courage; be not afraid, neither be thou dismayed: for the LORD thy God is with thee whithersoever thou goest."

Josh 1:6 - 9

Thrice in this text and in the same breath, God spoke to Joshua about courage. In verse 8, God shows us the place of grittiness by assigning Joshua a quotidian task.

"Be sure that the book of the Law is always read in your worship. Study it day and night, and make sure that you obey everything written in it. Then you will be prosperous and successful."

Josh 1:8(GNB)

In essence, the mundane precedes the marvellous; the extraordinary is made up of a large chunk of ordinary. But if you stick with it (whatever it may be), you are bound to make a success of it. Grittiness is the power behind the 10,000 hour rule.

Vision

"I will stand upon my watch, and set me upon the tower, and will watch to see what he will say unto me, and what I shall answer when I am reproved. 2 And the LORD answered me, and said, Write the vision, and make it plain upon tables, that he may run that readeth it."

Hab. 2:1- 2

Do you see the sequence in the metamorphosis of the vision as described by Prophet Habakkuk? First, it was audio-visual, then textual, then actual. All visions must go through this route before it becomes effective. An example of this model is the Lord Jesus himself. At His baptism by the hands of John, the Baptist in Jordan, the vision was both audio and visual: a voice spoke and the spirit in the form of a dove descended upon him (Luke 3:22). Much later, in the synagogue, the Lord read from Isaiah 61, then, the vision became textual. Why is this process of transcription and translation so important? Because it requires an attention to detail that promotes mastery. Certainly, you are familiar with the adage: "a picture is worth a thousand words". If you reverse engineer that adage, it might as well say "it takes a thousand words to paint a picture".

A little exercise – take a scene from the highpoint or low point of your day and translate it into a script. Describe in detail the emotions you felt, the ambience, the circumstance and the principal actors in that scene. Done? How long did it take you to produce the script? How long did the actual scene last? Did you notice that the effort to capture it all in text demanded that you give attention to details? This is also what happens when you write down a vision. Do you have a vision? Is it written down?

I found an interesting excerpt from Matthew Henry's commentary on the Habakkuk 2:1 text above: "The prophet humbly gives his attendance upon God (Hab.2:1): "I will stand upon my watch, as a sentinel on the walls of a besieged city, or on the borders of an invaded country, that is very solicitous to gain intelligence. I will look up, will look round, will look within, and watch to see what he will say unto me, will listen attentively to the words of his mouth and carefully observe the steps of his providence, that I may not lose the least hint of instruction or direction." This commentary describes multiple dimensions of vision: look up, look round and look within. To look up in aspiration, look around in appreciation and admiration of God's works; and look within in meditation. There is something about a well-articulated vision that gives the impetus for action.

"...let us run with patience the race that is set before us, 2 Looking unto Jesus..."

Even our Christian race is run as we look unto Jesus. The clearer we see Him, the easier the race gets.

In the early days of the space program, the National Aeronautical Space Agency (NASA), designed an experiment to determine the physiological and psychological effect of spatial disorientation on their astronauts. In the experiment, astronauts were made to wear specially fitted goggles which flipped their field of vision 180 degrees and turned their worlds upside down. The astronauts had to wear the goggles 24/7, even when they were asleep. It was observed that after a period of 26-30 days, though the astronauts continued to wear the goggles, their vision had turned right side up. The researchers therefore concluded that with a continuous stream of new input, the brain is able to form new neural pathways that make sense of the information it is fed with. What does this mean? Our vision affects our brain/mind, our perception and ultimately our reality. With a continuous stream of new information/code, the brain is able to declutter, debug, demystify and establish patterns in areas that previously seemed unconnected.

A couple of years ago, I was shopping for a car and I had my mind set on a particular brand of Toyota. Suddenly, this brand of car began to pop up everywhere I turned. It was as if everyone in my city was driving this very same brand. Was this the case? What really happened? What happened was that my desire and decision in favour of that brand of car, wired my brain to become consciously aware of the presence of those cars which had always been on the roads but that I was oblivious of.

As a wealth creator and accumulator, once your vision becomes clear and powerful enough, you begin to become aware of the opportunities available to attain it.

The 16th century sculptor, Michelangelo, famous for his marble sculpture of David was asked how he came to carve such a masterpiece. His response was that David was all the while in the marble stone, and that all he did was peel back the marble to reveal him. Such is the power of vision! Your masterpiece is caught, trapped in the pile of trash that clutters the world; do you have a vision of it powerful enough to unveil it?

Chameleons have the most distinctive eyes of any reptile. Each eye can pivot and focus independently, allowing the chameleon to observe two different objects simultaneously. Like the chameleon, the wealth creator or accumulator must be able to keep his eye on the game on multiple fronts or at least have staff that can do that while he/she keeps an eye on the staff

Chameleons are said to have the highest magnification per size of any vertebrate.35 Magnification is the process of enlarging the appearance, not the physical size of an object. It is related to scaling up images to be able to see more details. In essence, the chameleon can see more details per size of the object in its sight than any other vertebrate. This "attention to detail" is synonymous with words like meticulous, fastidious, exact, thorough, precise, fussy, painstaking etc. This is what wealth creation requires.

Chameleons can see in both visible and ultraviolet light. In contrast, the human eye can only see in the Red-Orange-Yellow-Green-Blue-Indigo-Violet (ROYGBIV) spectrum. Other spectra preceding the red colour (Infra- red) and the spectra after the violet colour (Ultraviolet) cannot be captured by the human eye. The wealth accumulator must be able to see beyond the spectra of human vision. This is akin to a supernatural perception that is promised to believers through the unction of Holy Spirit.

"There is so much more I want to tell you, but you can't bear it now. When the Spirit of truth comes, he will guide you into all truth. He will not speak on his own but will tell you what he has heard. He will tell you about the future"

John 16:12-13 NLT

A technology similar to seeing beyond the view of sight exists in the maritime and aviation industry with SONAR and RADAR technologies respectively. In both instances, wave generation and feedback is used to detect the presence of, and the approximate distance between objects. The wealth creator must know how to activate, perceive and rightly process information received from beyond the realm of sight.

Tongue

"Death and life are in the power of the tongue: and they that love it shall eat the fruit thereof."

Prov. 18:21

The Hebrew word translated as 'Power' is from the primitive word, yad which means hand. Thus life and death is in the hand of the tongue which means the tongue has the ability to grasp, handle, and take hold of. The writer of the book of James likens the tongue to a rudder, a spark of fire, a world of evil and deadly poison – powerful imageries to describe how something so little can affect something so great.

"Behold, we put bits in the horses' mouths, that they may obey us; and we turn about their whole body. 4 Behold also the ships, which though they be so great, and are driven of fierce winds, yet are they turned about with a very small helm, whithersoever the governor listeth. 5 Even so the tongue is a little member, and boasteth great things. Behold, how great a matter a little fire kindleth! 6 And the tongue is a fire, a world of iniquity: so is the tongue among our members, that it defileth the whole body, and setteth on fire the course of nature; and it is set on fire of hell... 8 But the tongue can no man tame; it is an unruly evil, full of deadly poison."

James 3:3 - 8

If we stick with the imagery of the "hand of the tongue", it means the tongue is ambidextrous! Life is in one hand; Death is in the other and the user has the ability to switch with ease between the two.

"Therewith bless we God, even the Father; and therewith curse we men, which are made after the similitude of God. 10 Out of the same mouth proceedeth blessing and cursing..."

James 3:9 - 10

As important as the hand is to the surgeon for precision in delivering healthcare, so is the tongue to man. The tongue is a precision tool. Hence, God's wisdom in giving us only one tongue in the midst of paired organs. Have you seen the movie, "Dr. Strange"? Why did the character quit surgery and become so frustrated? This is because he was involved in an accident which took away his surgical dexterity.

The tongue is as important in life and destiny as it is in wealth creation. Chameleons have a ballistic and highly extrudable tongue which reaches up to twice the length of their bodies. In the same vein, the believer who seeks to create wealth must reach out into the future and lay hold of it with the words of his mouth. We live in a voice activated world.

"Through faith we understand that the worlds were framed by the word of God, so that things which are seen were not made of things which do appear."

Heb. 11:3 KJV

Dr. Masaru Emoto, a Japanese scientist, describes the changes that occur to the crystalline structure of water simply by yelling at it! In his experiment, Dr. Emoto divided water into 100 petri dishes and assigned each a fate: good or bad. The good water was blessed or praised while the bad water was scolded continuously. At the end of his experiment, each petri dish was frozen and viewed under a microscope. The water which had been assigned a good fate by praise and blessing had rearranged itself into beautiful crystalline structure while the bad water had an ugly structure. Some other researchers have put forward arguments to debunk the claims made by Dr. Emoto, stating that the methodology of the experiment were not clearly stated or consistent which could account for the differences seen in the crystalline structure of the water.

These debates nonetheless, if Dr. Emoto's research is anything to go by, what have you been doing to the water constituents of your body? What kind of words have you been saying to your waters of health and wealth?

As of today, the world's population stands is in excess of 7 billion yet, no two individuals have the same voice not even identical twins or siblings. Each human voice is unique in frequency, amplitude and waveform. It is as unique as the iris and the finger prints. Such diversity in uniformity is God's signature within nature.

The voice is so unique that banks and security outfits are considering adding it as a security feature for their customers. In the same vein, our words can be a security feature for or against us.

"A fool's mouth is his destruction, and his lips are the snare of his soul"

Prov. 18:7

Words are so powerful such that even the second person of the Godhead is called The WORD.

CONCLUSION

This literary piece captures knowledge from history, life, living, nature, science, technology; relates with scriptural foundation and describes generic principles and strategies for wealth creation. The discussions are to make the wealth creation journey desirable, relatable and applicable to life and living. It is most desirable to inspire, influence and ultimately make wealth creation agenda common through massive and multiple income generation funnels and a purpose to establish His covenant and fulfil His will on earth.

No matter what estate you find yourself now, remember that God has created you to be a creator. You are as unique in your gifts and ability as you are in your iris, voice and fingerprints. Find something that resonates with you, something you are really passionate about and find a way to order it.

REFERENCES

1.https://en.wikipedia.org/wiki/List_of_countries_by_government_budget_(PPP)

2. http://www.investopedia.com/terms/p/parisclub.asp

3. http://www.clubdeparis.org/en

4. http://metro.co.uk/2015/07/03/here-are-the-worlds-biggest-charity-donors-were-talking-billions-5276452/

5. http://fortune.com/2015/07/01/saudi-prince-alwaleed-donation/

6. http://www.therichest.com/rich-list/world/the-10-richest-religions-in-the-world/

7. The 20 richest people of all time. Paola Bona/Shutterstock. www.msn.com

8. What are centrifugal and centripetal forces? Jim Lucas. www.livescience.com

9. Embryogenesis: www.en.m.wikipedia.org/wiki/Embryogenesis

10. Nuclear fission. www.britannica.com/science/nuclear-fission

11. Gather. www.wiktionary.orgaccessed via Livio andoird app

12. www.thebusinesspost.ng/economy/gas-flaring-nigeria-lost-710m-2016-nnpc

13. Gas flaring in Nigeria: problems and prospects, Global journal of politics and law research. www.eajournals.org

14. Negative effects of gas flaring: The Nigerian experience, 2013 (1)(1), Journal of Environmental pollution and human health, pg6

15. The Sun. www.en.m.wikipedia.org/wiki/sun

16. Guide to the sun. Phillips, K.J.H. (1995). Cambridge University press pg 47-53

17. Sun fact sheet. Williams, D.R. (2013). NASA Goddard space flight center

18. Physics in collision. Broggini, C. (2003). XXIII Physics in collision conference. Zeuthen, Germany. Pg 21

19. Ask us: Sun. Cosmicopia. NASA. 2012

20. Automation. Mikell P. Groover. www.britannica.com/technology/automation(Accessed on 27/9/2017

21.Billion-Dollar Bloodlines: America's Richest Families 2015. www.en.m.wikipedia.org/wiki/List_of_wealthiest_families

22. Walmart. www.en.m.wikipedia.org/wiki/walmart

23. Information for Walmart Investors unit counts & square footage. Retrieved February 21, 2017

24.List of largest companies by revenue www.en.m.wikipedia.org/wiki/List_of_largest_companies_by_revenue#List_of_largest_companies_by_revenue

25. Chameleon. www.a-z-animals.com/animals/chameleon/

26.10 Things you didn't know about chameleons. www.google.com.ng/amp/twistedsifter.com/2012/11/ten-things-you-didnt-know-about-chameleons/

27. The colourful language of chameleons. National Geographic (2015)

28. Dr. Strive Masiyiwa. www.facebook.com/stivemasiyiwa/

29. Common chameleon. Dever, Jennifer (2007)

30. The world's billionaires No 67 Aliko Dangote. www.forbes.com (2017)

31. Collocott, T. C. (ed.) (1974).Chambers Dictionary of science and technology.

Edinburgh: W. and R. Chambers. ISBN 0-550-13202-3

32."Omnivore-Biology-OnlineDictionary" www.biology-online.org. Retrieved 2016-04-02.

33.Angela Lee Duckworth

https://qz.com/work/1233940/angela-duckworth-explains-grit-is-the-key-to-success-and-self-confidence/

34 "Men of Honour" George Tillman Jr. 20th Century Fox

35 Ott, M., and F. Schaeffel. (1995).A negatively powered lens in the chameleon.Nature 373:692-694

36.Angela Lee Duckworth: Ted Talks Education
https://www.ted.com/talks/angela_lee_duckworth_grit_the_power_of_passion_and_perseverance/up-next?language=en

37. https://www.kenyaplex.com/resources/14494-theories-of-consumption.aspx ☐

RECOMMENDED READING

1) Blink by Malcolm Gladwell

2) Outliers by Malcolm Gladwell.

3) https://www.forbes.com/sites/margaretperlis/2013/10/29/5-characteristics-of-grit-what-it-is-why-you-need-it-and-do-you-have-it/#65277a2b4f7b

4) "Grit: ...success" by Angela Duckworth

5) The Millionaire Mind" and "The Millionaire Next Door" by Thomas J Stanley

6) "A whole new mind" by Daniel H. Pink

ABOUT THE AUTHOR

Jake is an avid learner and a student of life. He is a leadership, business and life coach; a serial entrepreneur and a consultant. He calls himself 'a bit of a futurist' because of his God-given ability to see beyond the curve and up to 10years down the line. He is married with children

.